SPANISH

Heather Leigh
and Salvador Ortiz-Carboneres

Illustrated by Joseph McEwan

Designed by Graham Round
Edited by Jane Chisholm

Contents

First published in 1980, with a different cover design.
This revised edition first published in 1987 by Usborne Publishing Ltd, 20 Garrick Street, London WC2E 9BJ, England.

Copyright © 1980, 1987 Usborne Publishing Ltd.

The name Usborne and the device are Trade Marks of Usborne Publishing Ltd.

Printed in Belgium.

How to use this Book

This book will help you make yourself understood in most everyday situations when you are on holiday or travelling in Spain. The phrases have been kept as simple as possible, and include some of the possible answers to the questions you may want to ask. There are also translations of many of the signs you will see.

The book is divided into sections, each covering a situation you are likely to find yourself in. Use the contents list at the front or the index at the back to help you find the pages you need. You will find it easier if you look up the section you are going to need in advance, so you can practise saying the phrases.

For most phrases, there is a picture with a speech bubble containing the Spanish. Underneath the picture is a guide to help you pronounce the Spanish and an English translation. Like this:

Hablo español.

Abloh espan-yoll.
I can speak Spanish

On the next two pages, you will find out how to use the pronunciation guide and there are some useful hints and phrases to remember. At the back of the book you can find some very basic Spanish grammar, including a few common verbs.

Points to remember

We have not always had enough space to include the words for "please" (*por favor*), or "excuse me" (*perdone*). Try to remember to add them when you are asking for things.

Por favor

There are four words in Spanish for "you" – *tú, vosotros, usted* and *ustedes*. *Tú* (singular) and *vosotros* (plural) are used by close friends and children. *Usted* (singular) and *ustedes* (plural) are for speaking to people you don't know very well. Be careful about using *tú* or *vosotros,* as people may think you are being rude.

Tú or Usted?

3

Pronunciation Guide

We have tried to keep the pronunciation guides in this book as simple as possible. For each Spanish sound we have used the English word, or part of a word, which sounds most like it. Read the pronunciation guide in what seems to be the most obvious way. It will sound better if you say it quickly, so it is a good idea to practise a bit. People should be able to understand what you are saying, even if you won't sound quite like a Spanish person. If you want to learn really good pronunciation you should try to find a Spanish person to teach you.

Here are some general points to remember when you are trying to speak Spanish.

A mark like this above a vowel is called a "stress mark". It means you should stress this part of the word more than the rest.

A mark like this above an "n" gives it a nasal sound, rather like "ny". Pronounce it as you would in the English word "new".

The Spanish "h" is never pronounced. All the other letters are pronounced, except the "u", which is sometimes silent.

Vowels, especially "o", sound better if you say them without closing your mouth at the end of the sound. Many consonants, such as "d", sound softer than in English.

The Spanish "r" is made by putting your tongue behind your top teeth. Think of the "r" in "grrr . . .!", the sound of a dog growling.

The Spanish "j" is a bit like an English "h". To pronounce it, you make a sound rather like the one you make when you gargle.

The letters "b" and "v" sound the same in Spanish. To pronounce them, make a sound half-way between the two.

In Spanish, "ll" is pronounced like the second part of the word "million", or like a "y", as in "yellow".

The Spanish "z" is pronounced "th". "C" also has a "th" sound, when it is followed by an "i" or an "e". Otherwise it is pronounced as in the English word "cat".

In Spanish "qu" sounds like "k", as the "u" is silent.

Some Basic Words and Phrases

Here are some useful words and phrases which you will need in all kinds of situations.

Sí
See
Yes

No
No
No

Por favor
Pour favorr
Please

Gracias
Grathee-ass
Thank you

Buenos días
Booenoss dee-ass
Good morning

Adiós
Addy-oss
Goodbye

Lo siento
Lo see-entoh
I'm sorry

Perdone
Peardonay
Excuse me

Señor
Sen-yorr
Mr

Señora
Sen-yorra
Mrs

Señorita
Sen-yorreeta
Miss

Some simple questions

How much? ¿Cuánto?
Cwantoe?

Why? ¿Por qué?
Pour kay?

Which one? ¿Cuál?
Cwal?

Where is . . .? ¿Dónde está . . .?
Donday esta . . .?

When? ¿Cuándo?
Cwandoe?

Have you? ¿Tiene usted . . .?
Tee-enay oo-sted . . .?

Is or are there . . .? Hay . . .?
¿Eye . . .?

Some simple statements

I am . . . Soy *or* Estoy . . .
Soy *or* Estoy . . .

I have . . . Tengo . . .
Tengo . . .

It is . . . Es or está . . .
Ess or esta . . .

It is here. Está aquí.
Esta a-key.

It is there. Está allí.
Esta eye-ee.

This one. Este.
Estay.

That one. Ese *or* aquél.
Essay *or* a-kell.

I would like . . . Me gustaría . . .
May goostar-reeya . . .

Problems with the language

Do you speak English?
¿Habla usted inglés?
Ab-la oo-sted ingless?

I do not speak Spanish
No hablo español.
No abloh espan-yoll.

I do not understand.
No entiendo.
No entee-endoh.

Please speak more slowly.
Más despacio, por favor.
Mass desspathy-oh pour favorr.

What does that mean?
¿Qué quiere decir?
Kay kee-airray deth-earr?

Finding your Way

La estatheeon, pour favorr.
How do I get to the station, please?

Tee-enay kay tomarr el out-oh-boos noomairroh thing-co.
You must take a number 5 bus.

Donday esta la pa-ra-da del out-oh-boos day El Es-corry-al?
Where is the bus stop for El Escorial?

Eye-ee. Ess a-kay-ya.
Over there. It's that one.

Ess esta la pa-ra-da day El Es-corry-al?
Is this where I get off for El Escorial?

Pour favorr. Donday esta el casteeyo?
Where is the castle, please?

Peardonay. May ay peardeedo. Com-o say ya-ma esta ky-yay?
Excuse me. I'm lost. What is the name of this street?

May lo ensenya en el ma-pa pour favorr?
Can you show me on the map?

General directions

Gire a la derecha.
Jeeray a la derecha.
Turn right.

Gire a la izquierda.
Jeeray a la
eethkee-airda.
Turn left.

Todo recto.
Tohdoh recktoh.
Straight on.

Está enfrente del cine.
Esta enfrentay del
theenay.
**It's opposite the
cinema.**

Está al lado del estanco.
Esta al lahdoh del
estangco.
**It's next to the
tobacconists.**

Está en la esquina.
Esta en la eskeena.
It's on the corner.

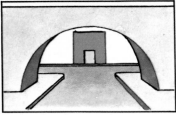

Está nada más pasar el puente.
Esta na-da mass pass-are el
pwentay.
It's just after the bridge.

Justo antes del cruce.
Hustoe antess del crewthay.
It's just before the crossroads.

Some places to ask for

la estación
la estatheeon
railway station

el aeropuerto
el airopwertoe
airport

la comisaría
la comisareeya
police station

el banco
el bangco
bank

las tiendas
lass tee-endass
the shops

At the Railway Station

¿Dónde se compran los billetes?

Allá, al fondo, en el despacho de billetes.

Donday say compran loss bee-yetess?
Where can I buy a ticket?

Eye-ya, al fondoe, en el despatchoe day bee-yetess.
Over there, at the ticket office.

¿Cuánto cuesta un billete para Madrid?

Un billete de ida para Madrid.

Dos billetes de ida y vuelta para Madrid.

Cwantoe cwesta oon bee-yetay pa-ra Madreeth?
How much is it to Madrid?

Oon bee-yetay day eeda pa-ra Madreeth.
One single ticket to Madrid.

Doss bee-yetess day eeda ee vwelta pa-ra Madreeth.
Two return tickets to Madrid.

¿De qué andén sale el tren para Madrid?

Andén número 5.

Day kay anden salay el tren pa-ra Madreeth?
Which platform does the Madrid train leave from?

Anden noomairroh thing-co.
Platform five.

¿A qué hora sale el tren?

Ah kay orra salay el tren?
What time does the train leave?

8

Ess estay el tren pa-ra Madreeth?
Is this the Madrid train?

Ay peardeedoh me bee-yetay!
I've lost my ticket!

Ah kay orra yay-ga el tren day Valentheea?
What time does the train from Valencia arrive?

Mohthoh!
Porter!

Information

Luggage collection

Waiting room

Lost property

Main line trains   **Suburban trains**

Left luggage

Not drinking water

It is dangerous to lean out of the window

Travelling by Car

Eye algoon garah-hay pour a-key?
Is there a garage near here?

Cwanta gasoleena kee-airray?
How much petrol do you want?

Yenayloe, pour favorr.
Fill it up please.

Pweday comprobar el athay-eetay ee el agwa?
Can you check the oil and water?

Ay teneedo oona avair-reeya.
I have broken down.

Kay lay passa?
What's the trouble?

Loss fraynoss no andan beeyen.
The brakes are not working properly.

Kee-airroh alkee-lar oon cochay pa-ra esta sem-ahna.
I would like to hire a car for the week.

Parts of the car

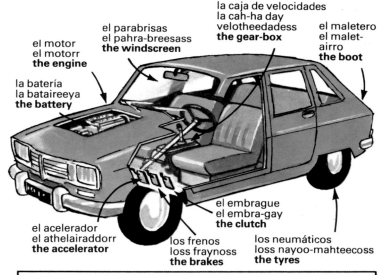

la caja de velocidades
la cah-ha day velotheedadess
the gear-box

el parabrisas
el pahra-breesass
the windscreen

el maletero
el malet-airro
the boot

el motor
el motorr
the engine

la batería
la bataireeya
the battery

el embrague
el embra-gay
the clutch

el acelerador
el athelairaddorr
the accelerator

los frenos
loss fraynoss
the brakes

los neumáticos
loss nayoo-mahteecoss
the tyres

Road signs

Found in forests and dry areas. Warns of the danger of fire.

Beware of the train.

Give way to other cars.

Restricted parking area. You need a blue disc to park here.

Motorway toll 1000m away.

Entrance to car park.

Town centre this way.

This shows you the coastal resorts you can get to from the next turn off.

At the Hotel

Hotels are graded from one to five stars, and prices are controlled by the government. You can get lists of hotels from a tourist office. Look out for *paradores* – first class hotels run by the government. These are often in converted castles or monasteries, or in places with beautiful scenery.

Booking in advance

Me gustaría reservar una habitación para la semana que viene.

May goostar-reeya resairvar oona abeetatheeon pa-ra la sem-ahna kay vee-enay.
I would like to book a room for next week.

Finding a room

Lo siento muchísimo, pero el hotel está completo.

Lo see-entoh moocheesy-mo, pear-o el ohtell esta completoh.
I'm sorry but the hotel is full.

¿Puede aconsejarme otro hotel?

Pweday aconsayhahmay oh-troe ohtell?
Can you recommend another hotel.

Una habitación con dos camas.

Oona abeetatheeon con doss camass.
A room with two beds.

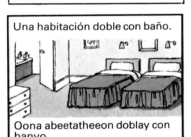

Una habitación doble con baño.

Oona abeetatheeon doblay con banyo.
A double room with bathroom.

Una habitación individual con ducha.

Oona abeetatheeon individ-ooal con doo-cha.
A single room with shower.

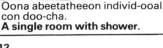

¿Cuánto tiempo piensa quedarse?

Cwantoe tee-empoh pee-ensa kaydarr-say?
How long will you be staying?

Hotel Meals

Lista de Precios

Habitación con desayuno
Bed and breakfast

Media pensión
Half board

Pensión completa
Full board

¿A qué hora sirven el desayuno (el almuerzo, la cena)?

A kay orra seer-ven el des-eye-oonoh (el almoo-airthoe, la thayna)?
What time is breakfast (lunch, dinner) served?

Huevos fritos
Oo-evoss freetoss
Fried eggs

Tostadas
Toh-star-dass
Toast

Chocolate con churros
Chocolahtay con chew-rross
Chocolate with fritters

¿Pueden prepararme la comida en bocadillos?

Pweden preparahmay la comeeda en bocka-deeyoss?
Could you make me a packed lunch?

Mi llave, por favor.

¿Cuál es el número de su habitación?

Me ya-vay pour favorr.
My key, please.

Cwal ess el noomairroh day soo abeetatheeon?
What is your room number?

Me gustaría dejar un recado para mi hermano.

May goostar-reeya dayhar oon reckahdoe pa-ra me airrmanoh.
I would like to leave a message for my brother.

Paying the bill

¿Podría prepararme la cuenta?

Podreea preparahmay la cwenta?
My bill, please.

13

Going Camping

There are over 500 campsites in Spain — mostly along the coast. They often have good facilities, such as swimming pools, sports areas, restaurants and supermarkets. You can get a list of approved campsites from the Spanish Tourist Office.

Finding a campsite

¿Se puede acampar aquí?

Say pweday a-camp-are a-key?
May we camp here?

Perdone. ¿Hay un camping cerca de aquí?

Peardonay. Eye oon campeeng therka day a-key?
Is there a campsite near here?

Tenemos una caravana y dos tiendas de campaña.

Tenaymoss oona ca-ra-vana ee doss tee-endass day campanya.
We have a caravan and two tents.

At the campsite

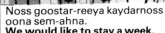

Nos gustaría quedarnos una semana.

Noss goostar-reeya kaydarnoss oona sem-ahna.
We would like to stay a week.

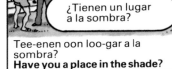

¿Tienen un lugar a la sombra?

Tee-enen oon loo-gar a la sombra?
Have you a place in the shade?

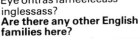

¿Hay otras familias inglesas?

Eye ohtras fameeleeass inglessass?
Are there any other English families here?

¿A qué hora cierran por la noche?

Ah kay orra thee-airran pour la nochay?
What time do you close at night?

14

¿Dónde me puedo lavar?

Donday may pwedoh lahvar?
Where can I wash?

¿Dónde hay agua?

Donday eye agwa?
Where can I find some water?

Perdone. ¿Puedo usar su linterna?

Peardonay. Pwedoh oosarr soo lintairr-na?
May I borrow your torch?

Perdone. ¿Podemos encender una hoguera?

Peardonay. ¿Podaymoss enthendair oona ogairra?
Are we allowed to make a camp fire?

¿Qué es ese olor?

Kay ess essay olorr?
What is that smell?

Por favor. ¿Pueden hacer un poco menos de ruido?

Pour favorr. Pweden athair oon pohcoh menoss day roo-eedoh?
Please could you make less noise.

What the signs mean

SE PROHIBE FREGAR LOS PLATOS EN LOS LAVABOS.
No washing up in the basins.

APARCAMIENTO OBLIGATORIO
Compulsory parking

AGUA POTABLE
Drinking water

RESERVADO PARA CARAVANAS
Caravans only

SE RUEGA A LOS CAMPISTAS ECHEN LA BASURA EN LOS RECIPIENTES PREVISTOS PARA TAL FUNCION.
Campers are requested to dispose of their rubbish in the places provided.

Going Shopping

Most Spanish shops are open from 9.00 a.m. to 7.00 p.m. They close for a long lunch break between 1.00 p.m. and 4.00 p.m. Big department stores are usually open at lunchtime, but they open later in the morning and close earlier in the evening.

Peardonay, donday pwedoh comprarr froota?
Where can I buy some fruit?

Tee-enay manthan-ass?
Have you any apples?

Cwantass kee-airray?
How many would you like?

Oon keeloe.
A kilo.

Cwatroe long-has day ham-on pour favorr.
Four slices of ham, please.

Estoy me-randoe.
I am just looking.

Signs

Sale

Self service

ASCENSOR
Lift

Abierto de las 9 a las 6·30
Open from 9 a.m. to 6.30 p.m.

16

Buying clothes

¿Haría el favor de enseñarme una camisa estampada?

Ahreeya el favorr day ensenyarmay oona cameesa estam-pada?
Can you help me? I am looking for a patterned shirt.

Sí. ¿Qué talla desea?

See. Kay tie-ya dessay-a?
Yes. What size do you want?

¿Puedo probármela?

Pwedoh probarmayla?
May I try it on?

Es demasiado grande.

Es demasiado pequeña.

Es dem-assee-addoh granday.
It's too big.

Es dem-assee-addoh pek-ayn-ya.
It's too small.

¿Cuánto es?

Cwantoe ess?
How much is it?

¿Tienen algo más barato?

Tee-enen algo mass ba-ratoh?
Have you anything cheaper?

¿Dónde pago?

Donday pag-oh?
Where do I pay?

Gracias.

De nada.

Grathee-ass.
Thank you.

Day na-da.
You are welcome.

17

The Shops 1

Ultramarinos - Alimentación
Ooltra-mareenoss - Alleementatheeon **Grocers**

Querría . . .

Care-reeya . . .
I would like . . .

conservas
con-sair-vass
tinned foods

queso
kayzoh
cheese

mantequilla
mantay-keeya
butter

huevos
oo-ev-oss
eggs

mermelada
mair-mel-adder
jam

té
tay
tea

leche
laychay
milk

azúcar
a-thoo-car
sugar

galletas
ga-yet-ass
biscuits

miel
me-ell
honey

mostaza
mos-tath-a
mustard

café
caf-ay
coffee

judías verdes
who-deeass vair-dess
green beans

guisantes
geese-antess
peas

coliflor
collyfloor
cauliflower

patatas
pa-ta-tass
potatoes

lechuga
le-chew-ga
lettuce

champiñones
champin-yoness
mushrooms

col
col
cabbage

tomates
tom-at-ess
tomatoes

cebollas
thebo-yass
onions

frambuesas
framboo-esass
raspberries

un limón
oon lee-mon
a lemon

manzanas
manthan-ass
apples

peras
pear-ass
pears

una naranja
oona na-ranha
an orange

ciruelas
theerooay-lass
plums

plátanos
plat-a-noss
bananas

fresas
fressass
strawberries

18

CARNICERÍA

Carneethair-reeya
Butcher

carne picada de vaca
carnay pikada day va-ca
minced beef

un pollo
oon po-yo
a chicken

un bistec
oon beestek
a steak

chuletas
de cordero
chew-letass
day cordairro
lamb chops

Charcutería

Sharcootair-reeya
Pork Butcher

longanizas
longan-eethass
sausages

chuletas de cerdo
chew-letass day
thairdoe
pork chops

foie gras
fwa-gra
paté

salchichón
salcheechon
salami

entremeses
entray-messess
**prepared salads
and cooked meats**

Panadería

Panaddair-reeya
Baker

unos bollos
oonoss bo-yos
some rolls

pan
pan
bread

una barra de pan
oona barra day pan
a long loaf

PASTELERÍA

Pastelair-reeya
Cake and Sweet Shop

una tarta de frutas
oona tarta day frootass
a fruit tart

unos caramelos
oonass ca-rramelloss
some sweets

un pastel
oon passtell
a cake

PESCADERÍA

Pescadair-reeya
Fishmonger

lenguado
leng-gwa-doe
sole

una gamba
oona gamba
a prawn

merluza
mair-lootha
hake

bacalao
back-allow
cod

The Shops 2
Librería · Papelería · Kiosco

Leebrair-reeya – Papelair-reeya – Key-oskoe
Bookshop – Stationers – Newspaper kiosk

tinta
tin-ta
ink

un bolígrafo
oon bollygraffoh
a ballpoint

un libro
oon leebroe
a book

una goma
oona gom-a
a rubber

un periódico
oon perryoddy-coe
a newspaper

sobres
so-brays
envelopes

un lápiz
oon lapeeth
a pencil

ESTANCO

Estangco
Tobacconist

papel para cartas
papel pa-ra cartass
writing paper

un mechero
oon may-chair-roe
a lighter

un paquete de cigarrillos
oon packetay day theegarree-oss
a packet of cigarettes

cerillas
ther-ee-yas
matches

sellos
say-yoss
stamps

boutique

Booteek
Clothes Shop

una camisa
oona cameesa
a shirt

un sombrero
oon sombrairroh
a hat

unos pantalones cortos
oonoss pantal-oness cor-toss
some shorts

una falda
oona falda
a skirt

un vestido
oon vesteedoe
a dress

unos zapatos
oonoss thapatoss
some shoes

unas sandalias
oonass sandall-yass
some sandals

un jersey
oon hair-say
a jersey

unos pantalones
oonoss panta-lone-ays
some trousers

un traje de baño
oon trah-hay day ban-yo
a bathing costume

un impermeable
oon im-pear-me-ablay
a raincoat

FERRETERÍA

Fair-retair-reeya
Ironmongers-Hardware Store

un abrelatas
oon abray-la-tass
a tin opener

una linterna
oona lintairr-na
a torch

un destornillador
oon destornee-yadoor
a screwdriver

un sacacorchos
oon sack-a-corchoss
a corkscrew

una pila
oona peel-a
a battery

una bombilla
oona bom-bee-ya
a light bulb

cuerda
cwairda
string

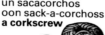

unas tijeras
oonass tee-hair-ass
some scissors

detergente
det-airr-hentay
some detergent

hilo
eel-oh
cotton

una aguja
oona agoo-ha
a needle

un enchufe
oon enchewfay
a plug

gas
gas
Camping gas

FARMACIA

Farmatheeya
Chemist

aspirinas
asspeareenass
aspirins

una venda
oona ven-da
a bandage

insecticida
insecteetheeda
insect repellent

jabón
ha-bon
soap

polvos de talco
pol-voss day tal-co
talcum powder

pasta de dientes
passtah day dee-entess
toothpaste

un cepillo de dientes
oon thep-eeyo day dee-entess
a toothbrush

una película
oona peleek-oola
a film

unas tiritas
oonass tiree-tass
sticking plaster

un peine
oon pay-e-nay
a comb

un rollo de papel higiénico
oon rohyo day papel ee-hyen-icoe **a roll of toilet paper**

Posting a Letter . . .

The post office is called *Correos y Telégrafos*. It is open from 9 a.m. to 1.30 p.m. and from 4 p.m. to 7 p.m. from Monday to Saturday. You can buy stamps from an *estanco*, or tobacconist's, too. To post letters abroad, look for a box marked *extranjero*.

Perdone. ¿Cuánto es para Inglaterra?

Perdonay. Cwantoe ess pa-ra Inglatairra?
Excuse me. How much is it to England?

Quiero cuatro sellos para Inglaterra.

Key-airroh cwatroe say-yoss pa-ra Inglatairra.
I would like four stamps to England.

Perdone. ¿Dónde hay un buzón?

Peardonay. Donday eye oon boothon?
Excuse me, where can I find a postbox.

The post office

¿Dónde está Correos?

Donday esta corray-oss?
Where is the post office?

Quiero mandar un telegrama a Inglaterra.

Key-airroh man-darr oon telaygrama ah Inglatairra.
I would like to send a telegram to England.

Rellene este formulario, por favor.

Reh-yaynay estay formoolahreeo, pour favorr.
Fill in this form, please.

¿Cuánto es por palabra?

Cwantoe ess pour pal-abra?
How much is it per word?

. . . and Changing Money

¿Cuánto es el franqueo de este paquete para Inglaterra?

Cwantoe ess el frankayoh day estay pah-ketay pa-ra Inglatairra?
How much will it cost to send this parcel to England?

¿A qué hora es la última recogida de correo?

Ah kay orra ess la oolteema reh-coh-heeda day corray-oh?
What time does the last post leave?

Signs

POR AVIÓN

Air mail

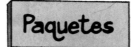

Paquetes

Parcels

TELEGRAMAS

Telegrams

SELLOS

Postage stamps

Changing money

You can change money and traveller's cheques in a bank, a *cambio* (exchange office) and in some hotels and railway stations. Remember to take your passport with you. Banks are usually open from 9.00 a.m. to 2.00 p.m. *Cambios* are open for longer – sometimes even on Sundays.

Perdone, ¿cambian cheques de viaje?

Peardonay, cam-beean check-ays day veeah-hay?
Excuse me, do you cash traveller's cheques?

¿A cuánto está la libra?

Ah cwanto esta la lee-bra?
How many pesetas are there to the pound?

Por favor, podría darme el cambio en monedas.

Pour favorr, podreea darrmay el cambeeoh en mon-aidass.
Could I have some small change.

Going to a Café

Cafés in Spain stay open from early in the morning to very late at night. You can buy snacks and both alcoholic and non-alcoholic drinks. Many cafés have tables outside, because of the warm climate. Look out for *tapas*, titbits served at the bar to eat with your drinks.

¿Está ocupada?

Esta ocoo-pa-da?
Is this table taken?

¿Qué desean?

Kay dessayan?
What can I get you?

¿Por favor, puede traernos la carta?

Pour favorr, pweday try-airnoss la carta?
Please may we see the menu.

¿Qué bocadillos tienen?

Jamón, queso y salchichón.

Kay bocka-deeyoss tee-enen?
What sandwiches have you got?

Ham-on, kayzoh ee salcheechon.
Ham, cheese and salami.

Yo quiero dos bocadillos de jamón, una Coca-Cola y un zumo de naranja.

Yo key-airroh doss bocka-deeyoss day ham-on, oona cocka coala ee oon thoomoh day na-ranha.
I would like two ham sandwiches, a Coca-Cola and an orange juice.

24

Un tenedor, por favor.

Oon tenedorr, pour favorr.
A fork, please.

Yo no he pedido esto.

Yo no ay pedee-doh estoh.
I didn't order this.

Un cuchillo
Oon coocheeyo
A knife

Una jarra de agua
Oona harra
day agwa
A jug of water

Una cuchara
Oona coochara
A spoon

Un vaso
Oon vahsoh
A glass

Una servilleta
Oona sairveeyeta
A napkin

Sal y pimienta
Sal ee peamy-
enta
Salt and pepper

¿Dónde están los servicios?

Donday es-tan loss
sairveetheeoss?
Where are the toilets?

¡Camarero!

Cama-rair-roh!
Waiter!

La cuenta, por favor.

La cwenta, pour favorr.
The bill, please.

¿Está el servicio
incluido?

Esta el sairveetheeoh in-clue-
eedoh?
Is service included?

Going to a Restaurant

Spanish restaurants are divided into categories indicated by the number of forks shown outside – from one to five. Look out for restaurants called *fondas*, *posadas* or *ventas*. These offer good simple meals at reasonable prices.

Querría reservar una mesa para cuatro a las ocho de la noche.

Care-reeya resairvarr oona messa pa-ra cwatroe a lass och-oh day la nochay.
I would like to book a table for four at 8 p.m.

¿Tiene una mesa para cuatro?

Tee-enay oona messa pa-ra cwatroe?
Have you a table for four?

¿Ha reservado?

Ah resairrvadoe?
Have you booked?

¿Tiene una mesa fuera?

Tee-enay oona messa fooaira?
Have you a table outside?

¿Qué desean ustedes?

Kay dessayan oo-stedays?
What would you like to order?

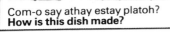

¿Cómo se hace este plato?

Com-o say athay estay platoh?
How is this dish made?

¿Tiene algo muy sencillo?

Tee-enay algo mwee sentheeyo?
Have you got anything plainer?

Drinks

¿Puedo ver la lista de vinos?

Pwedoh vair la leesta day vee-noss?
Could I see the wine list?

¿Qué me aconseja?

Kay may a-consay-ha?
What do you recommend?

Quiero una jarra de vino de la casa y una botella de agua mineral.

Key-airroh oona harra day vee-noh day la ca-sa ee oona bott-ay-ya day agwa minairral.
I would like a carafe of house wine and a bottle of mineral water.

¿Qué tiene sin alcohol?

Kay tee-enay sin alcoh-ol?
What soft drinks have you got?

Lo siento mucho, se me ha volcado el vaso.

Lo see-entoh moochoh, say may ah volcah-doh el vahsoh.
I'm sorry, I've spilt my drink.

Tenemos un poco de prisa.

Tenaymoss oon pohcoh day preesa.
We are in a bit of a hurry.

Problems with the bill

Perdone. ¿Qué quiere decir esto?

Peardonay. Kay kee-airray deth-earr estoh?
Excuse me. What does this mean?

The Menu

Churros
Chew-rross
Fritters

Jamón
Ham-on
Ham

Tostadas
Toss-tardass
Toast

Queso
Kayzoh
Cheese

Mantequilla y confitura
Mantay-keeya ee
confeetourra
Butter and jam

Paella
Pie-ay-ya
Rice dish

Bocadillo
Bockadee-yo
Sandwich

Chorizo
Choh-rreethoh
Spicy sausage

Ensalada
Ensa-ladda
Salad

Tortilla
Torr-teeya
Omelette

Restaurant Menu

Keep a look out for restaurants which have a special set menu, called a
Plato Combinado, Menú Turístico or a *Menú del Día.* This is cheaper
than choosing from the ordinary menu. *Vino Incluido* means that wine
is included in the price.

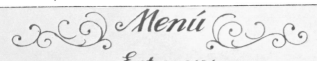

Menú

Entremeses
Starters

Embutidos
Embooteedos
Pork meats

Mariscos
Mareesscoss
Shellfish

Aceitunas
A-thay-too-nass
Olives

Gambas
Gambass
Prawns

Mejillones
Meh-he-yoness
Mussels

Cigalas
Thee-galess
Crayfish

Ostras
Ostrass
Oysters

Sopa
Soup

Gazpacho
Gathpatchoh
Chilled vegetable soup

Sopa de ajo
Sohpa day a-hoh
Garlic soup

Patatas fritas
Pa-ta-tass freetass
Chips

Café solo
Cafay solo
Black coffee

Helado
Ell-addoh
Ice cream

Café con leche
Cafay con lechay
White coffee

Pasteles
Pastelless
Cakes

Té con leche
Tay con lechay
Tea with milk

Pinchitos
Pincheetoss
Kebabs

Chocolate caliente
Chocolahtay
calee-entay
Hot chocolate

Hamburguesa
Amburrguessa
Hamburger

Zumo de naranja
Thoomoh day
na-ranha
Orange juice

Carne
Meat

Cochinillo asado
Cochineeyo a-sahdoh
Roast suckling pig

Cocido
Cotheedoh
Meat and bean casserole

Verduras y legumbres
Vegetables

Pescado
Fish

Lenguado
Len-gwadoh
Sole

Trucha
Troocha
Trout

Zarzuela
Tharrthooayla
Spicy fish stew

Postre
Last course

Fruta
Froota
Fruit

Tarta de Manzana
Tarta day manthana
Apple tart

Queso
Kayzoh
Cheese

Entertainments 1

To find out what is on in the area, look in a local paper, or ask at the nearest tourist office (*Oficina de Turismo*). If you are staying in a hotel, the receptionist may be able to help. When you go to the cinema or the theatre, you are expected to tip the usherette.

¿Hay algún espectáculo bueno?

Eye algoon espectak-ooloh booenoh?
Can you recommend a show to see?

Circo
Theerco
Circus

Teatro de Marionetas
Tayatroh day Marryon-etass
Puppet Theatre

Una Película de Dibujos Animados
Oona Peleek-oola day Deeboohoss Aneemahdoss
Cartoon Film

Teatro al Aire Libre
Tayatroh al Eye-ray Leebray
Open-Air Theatre

Un Parque de Atracciones
Oon Parkay day At-track-theeoness
A Fairground

Una Pantomima
Oona Pantomeema
A Pantomime

Luz y Sonido
Looth ee Soneedoh
Sound and Light Show
(These tell the story of famous old buildings in which they are held.)

Un Prestidigitador
Oon Presteedee-hitahdoor
A Magician

Un Partido de Fútbol
Oon Parteedoh day Footboll
A Football Match

¿Qué ponen esta noche en el cine?

Kay pon-en esta nochay en el theenay?
What is on at the cinema tonight?

¿Hay una película en inglés?

Eye oona peleek-oola en ingless?
Is there a film in English?

¿Cuánto es?

Dos butacas.

Cwantoe ess?
How much are the tickets?

Doss bootackass
Two seats in the stalls.

1 El Patio de Butacas
El Pateeoh day Bootackass
The Stalls

2 El Gallinero
El Gah-yeenairro
The Gallery

3 El Anfiteatro
El Anfee-tayatroh
The Dress Circle

4 Los Palcos
Loss Palcoss
Boxes

Entertainments 2

¿A qué hora empieza el espectáculo?

A las seis y media. Termina a las ocho.

Ah kay orra empee-etha el espectak-ooloh?
What time does the show begin?

Ah lass say-eess ee meddy-a. Tear-meena ah lass och-oh.
At six-thirty p.m. It finishes at eight p.m.

¿Dónde puedo comprar un programa?

Donday pwedoh comprarr oon program-a?
Where can I buy a programme?

La acomodadora los vende.

La acomoddadorr-a loss venday.
The usherette sells them.

Theatre signs

EL GUARDARROPA

Cloakroom

Salida de Emergencia

Fire exit

SERVICIOS

Toilets

PROHIBIDO FUMAR

No smoking

ÚNICAMENTE MAYORES 18 AÑOS

This sign means that children under the age of 18 are not allowed to see the show.

Sightseeing 1

The *Oficina de Turismo* will also give you sightseeing information. You will sometimes have to pay an entrance fee to visit places of interest. Museums are often closed, for all or half the day, on Mondays. A few places are closed during the winter.

¿Qué hay de interés en la ciudad?

Kay eye day interress en la thew-dath?
What is there of interest to see in the town?

Places to go sightseeing

El Castillo
El Casteeyo
The Castle

El Zoológico
El Thoo-oloh-heeko
The Zoo

El Museo
El Moosayoh
The Museum

La Iglesia
La Iglesseeya
The Church

El Barrio Antiguo
El Barryo Anteegwo
Old Part of Town

Parque Nacional
Parkay Natheeonarl
National Park

Las Cuevas
Lass Cwevass
Caves

¿Hay un mapa turístico de la ciudad?

Eye oon ma- pa too-reesteeko day la thew-dath?
Is there a tourist map of the town?

¿Puede decirme cuándo está abierto el museo?

Pweday dethearrmay cwandoe esta abby-airtoh el moosayoh?
Can you tell me when the museum is open?

Todos las días, excepto los lunes, desde las 9 hasta la 1.

Todoss loss dee-ass, ectheptoh loss looness, desday lass noo-evay hasta la oona.
Every day, except Monday, from 9 a.m. to 1 p.m.

¿Cuánto es la entrada?

Cwantoe ess la entrahda?
How much is the admission charge?

33

Sightseeing 2

Guided tours

¿Hay una visita con guía en inglés?

Eye oona veeseeta con geea en ingless?
Is there a guided tour in English?

Sí. La próxima visita empieza dentro de un cuarto de hora.

See. La proxeema veeseeta empee-etha dentro day oon cwarto day orra.
Yes the next tour starts in a quarter of an hour.

¿Cuánto dura la visita?

Cwantoe doora la veeseeta?
How long does the tour last?

¿Se puede subir a la torre?

Say pweday soo-beer ah la torray?
Can one go up the tower?

At the zoo

La Casa de Reptiles
La Cassa day Reptee-less
Reptile House

La Jaula de los Pájaros
La Howla day loss Pah-harross
The Aviary

Los Monos
Loss Monoss
Monkey House

La Merienda de los Chimpancés
La Meree-enda day loss Chimp-anthess
Chimpanzees Tea Party

El Foso de los Osos
El Fossoh day loss Ossoss
Bear Pit

Paseos en Burro
Passayos en Boorroh
Donkey rides

Paseos en Camello
Passayos en Cam-ay-yo
Camel rides

34

Signs

Do not feed the Animals

Dangerous Animals

Wild Animals

Entrance

Exit

Do not Touch

Cameras Prohibited

Tea-Room

Private Property

Beware of the Dog

No Entrance

Closed for the Holidays

Open

Closed

Keep off the Grass

Making Friends

Hola. ¿Cómo te llamas?

Me llamo María. ¿Y tú?

Oh-la. Com-o tay yamass?
Hello. What is your name?

May ya-mo Ma-rreea. Ee too?
My name is Maria. And yours?

Vivo allí.

¿Dónde vives?

Donday veevess?
Where are you staying?

Veevoh eye-ee.
I live over there.

¿Cuántos años tienes?

Tengo doce años.

Cwantoss an-yoss tee-eness?
How old are you?

Tengo dothay an-yoss.
I'm 12.

Éste es mi hermano Juan. ¿Tienes hermanos o hermanas?

Estay ess mee airrmanoh Hooan. Tee-eness airrmanoss oh airrman-ass?
This is my brother Juan. Have you any brothers or sisters?

Sí. Tengo una hermana mayor. Y éste es mi hermano gemelo.

See. Tengo oona airrmana my- orr. Ee estay ess me airrmanoh hem-ello.
Yes. I have an elder sister. And here is my twin brother.

¿Puedes comer con nosotros?

Pwedess comair con noss-otross?
Can you have lunch with us?

Tengo que preguntar a mis padres.

Tengo kay praygoontarr ah mees pah-dress.
I must ask my parents.

¡Vamos a jugar!

Va-moss ah hoo-garr.
Let's go and play.

¡Date prisa!

¡Espérame!

¡Ya voy!

Dahtay preesa!
Hurry up!

Ya voy!
I'm coming!

Espearra-may!
Wait for me!

Me gusta . . .

May goosta . . .
I like . . .

El ajedrez
El a-headrreth
Chess

Pintar
Pintarr
Painting

La Filatelia
La Feelatell-eea
Stamp Collecting

Cards

Oros
Oh-ross
Diamonds

Copas
Coh-pass
Hearts

Bastos
Basstoss
Clubs

Espadas
Espah-dass
Spades

El Rey
El Ray
King

La Reina
La Rayeena
Queen

La Sota
La Sohta
Jack

El As
El Ass
Ace

El Comodín
El Coh-moh-deen
Joker

Playing Games

¡Te toca a ti!

¡Ve a buscarla!

Vay ah booscarrlah!
Go and get it!

Tay tocka ah tee!
It's your turn!

Juego del escondite
Hooay-goh del escondeetay
Hide and Seek

Montar en bicicleta
Montarr en beetheekleta **Bicycling**

¡Tírame el balón!

¡Cógelo!

Tier-ramay el bal-on!
Throw me the ball!

Coh-hayloh!
Catch!

A la pata coja.
Ah la pa-ta co-ha.
Hopscotch

Sports

There is a lot of good fishing in Spain, especially for salmon, trout, pike and carp. For fishing in lakes and rivers, you need a permit, for which you will have to pay, from the *Delegación de Turismo* in the province concerned.

Going fishing

¿Dónde puedo alquilar una caña de pescar?

Donday pwedoh alkee-lar oona can-ya day pess-carr?
Where can I hire a fishing rod?

¿Cuánto es por día?

Cwantoe ess pour deea?
How much does it cost for the day?

¿Necesito un permiso?

Nethess-eetoh oon pear-meesoh?
Must one have a permit?

Perdone. ¿Tiene usted cebo para pescar?

Peardonay. Tee-enay oo-sted thay-boh pa-ra pess-carr?
Have you any bait, please?

¿Es un buen sitio para pescar?

Ess oon booen seatee-oh pa-ra pess-carr?
Is this a good place to fish?

Riding

¿Se puede montar a caballo por aquí?

Say pweyday montarr ah cab-eye-yo pour a-key?
Can one go riding near here?

Querríamos unas lecciones de equitación.

Kair-ree-amoss oonass lecthee-ownays day eh-keytatheeon.
We would like some riding lessons.

Skiing

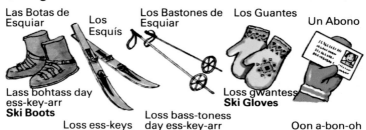

Las Botas de Esquiar
Lass bohtass day ess-key-arr
Ski Boots

Los Esquís
Loss ess-keys
Skis

Los Bastones de Esquiar
Loss bass-toness day ess-key-arr
Ski Sticks

Los Guantes
Loss gwantess
Ski Gloves

Un Abono
Oon a-bon-oh
Ski Pass

¿Dónde está la escuela de esquí?

Donday esta la es-cwela day ess-key?
Where is the ski school?

The ski runs

The ski runs, or Pistas, are marked with coloured arrows.

Nursery slopes— very easy.

Beginners—easy.

For quite experienced skiers—quite difficult.

For professional skiers— very difficult.

Soy principiante.

Soy printhee-pee-antay.
I am a beginner.

Yo ya he esquiado una vez.

Yoh ya ay ess-key-addoh oona veth.
I have skied once before.

Sé esquiar bien.

Say ess-key-arr beeyen.
I can ski well.

No puedo levantarme. ¿Puede ayudarme?

No pwedoh lev-antarr-may. Pweday ay-oodarr-may?
I cannot get up. Can you help me?

Nos hemos perdido. ¿Dónde está el telesquí?

Noss ay-moss peardeedoh. Donday esta el telesskey?
We are lost. Where is the ski-lift?

At the Seaside 1

Donday esta la ply-a mass thair-cana?
Where is the nearest beach?

Eye oona peas-theena?
Is there a swimming pool?

Key-airroh alkee-lar doss colchon-etass, oona amaca . . .
I would like to hire two mattresses, a deck chair . . .

. . . ee oona sombree-ya.
. . . and a parasol.

¿Donday pwedoh cambee-arrmay?
Where are the changing rooms?
Al lahdoh day la peas-theena pa-ra neen-yoss.
Next to the paddling pool.

Beach things

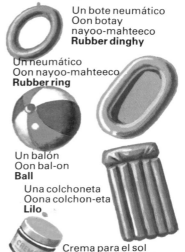

Un bote neumático
Oon botay nayoo-mahteeco
Rubber dinghy

Un neumático
Oon nayoo-mahteeco
Rubber ring

Un balón
Oon bal-on
Ball

Una colchoneta
Oona colchon-eta
Lilo

Crema para el sol
Krayma pa-ra el sol
Suntan cream

Hola. ¿Vamos a nadar?

Oh-la. Va-moss ah nahdarr?
Hello. Let's go for a swim.

Por favor, ¿puede cuidarme mis cosas?

Pour favorr, pweday cwee-darrmay mees coss-ass?
Please could you look after my things for me?

¡Cuidado! ¡Viene una ola grande!

Cweedahdoh! Vee-enay oona olla granday!
Watch out! There's a big wave coming!

¿Hay una ducha?

Eye oona doo-cha?
Is there a shower?

Páseme la toalla.

Pahsaymay la toh-eye-ya.
Pass me the towel.

El Esquí Acuático
El Esskey Ahquahteeco
Water skiing

Pedalo
Peh-dah-loh
Pedalo

Un Barco de Vela
Oon Barr-coh day Vayla
Sailing boat

At the Seaside 2

¿Hacemos un castillo de arena?

¿Tienes un cubo y una pala?

A-thaymoss oon casteeyo day ah-rayna?
Shall we build a sand castle?
Tee-eness oon coobo ee oona pahla?
Have you got a bucket and spade?

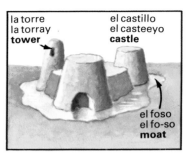

la torre
la torray
tower

el castillo
el casteeyo
castle

el foso
el fo-so
moat

¿Qué significa la bandera roja?

Kay signeefeeka la bandairra roha?
What does the red flag mean?

Es peligroso nadar. El mar está agitado.

PROHIBIDO BAÑARSE

Ess pelee-grosso nahdarr. El marr esta a-hee-tahdoh.
It is dangerous to swim. The sea is too rough.

No Bathing

Tengo calor.

Tengo cal-orr.
I'm hot.

Vamos a comprar un helado.

Va-moss ah comprarr oon elladdoh.
Let's go and buy an ice cream.

Accidents and Emergencies

You can find the numbers for fire, police and ambulance services on the wall inside a public telephone box. Road accidents should be reported to the police station (*Comisaría*). If you are in serious trouble, contact a British Consulate.

¡Socorro!

Soh-coh-rroh!
Help!

¡Vengan pronto!

Veng-gann pronto!
Come quickly!

¡Fuego!

Foo-eggoh!
Fire!

Por favor, llamen una ambulancia.

Pour favorr, ya-men oona amboolantheea.
Please call for an ambulance.

Missing persons

Mi amigo falta desde anoche.

Me ameegoh fal-ta desday a-nochay.
My friend has been missing since last night.

¿Cúando lo vio por última vez?

¿Cwandoe lo veeoh pour oolteema veth?
When did you last see him?

Salió a las seis a comprar un periódico.

Sallyo a lass sayeess a comprarr oon perryoddy-coe.
He went out at 6.00 p.m. to buy a newspaper.

Llevaba una bufanda y un sombrero rojos.

Yev-ah-ba oona boofanda ee oon sombrairroh roh-hoss.
He was wearing a red hat and scarf.

Lost or stolen

He perdido mi pasaporte.

Ay peardeedoh me passa- portay.
I have lost my passport.

Me han robado el billetero

May an robaddoh el beeyetairro.
My wallet has been stolen.

Han entrado a robar en mi habitación.

An entrahdoh ah rohbarr en me abeetatheeon.
My room has been burgled.

¿Dónde podemos ponernos en con- tacto con usted?

Donday podaymoss ponairnoss en contactoh con oo-sted.
Where can we contact you.

Other things

mis cheques de viaje
mees checkess day veeah-hay
my traveller's cheques

mi cámara fotografica
me ca-mara fotografee- cah
my camera

mi maleta
me malet-a
my suitcase

mis llaves
mees ya-vess
my keys

mi bolso
me bolsoh
my bag

mi reloj
me rel-ohh
my watch

Pasó entre las diez de la noche y mediodía.

Passoh entray lass dee-eth day la nochay ee meddy-oh-deea.
It happened between 10.00 p.m. and midday.

Aquí tiene mi nombre y dirección.

A-key tee-enay me nombray ee dee-recktheeon.
Here is my name and address.

Using the Telephone

In Spain you can find public telephones in many cafés and shops, or you could look for a telephone box, or *cabina telefónica*. The telephone system works independently of the post office, so you will not find telephones there. If you want to make long distance calls, or look up numbers in the directories, you could go to the telephone exchange, or *central telefónica*.

Most telephones are coin-operated. You can use either 5, 25, or 50 peseta pieces. Before dialling, you line up the coin or coins in a rack above the dial. When you have dialled the number, you should hear a series of rapid pips. This is the ringing tone. When the call is answered, one of the coins will fall into a slot. When the time runs out, another coin will fall in.

Many telephone boxes are for local calls only. To call another town or country, look for a box with a green strip across the top, marked *"interurbano"*.

Making a phone call

Perdone, ¿puedo usar su teléfono?

Peardonay, pwedoh oosarr soo tel-efonoh?
Please may I use the telephone?

Por favor, ¿puede darme cambio?

Pour favorr, pweday darrmay cambee-oh?
Please could you give me some change?

Quiero poner una conferencia para Londres, a cobro revertido. El número es 800 6009.

Key-airroh pon-airr oonah confair-entheea pa-ra Londress ah cob-rroh reh-vairteedoh. El noomairroh ess 800 6009.
I want to call London and reverse the charges. The number is London 800 6009.

Cwal ess soo noomairroh?
No cwel-gay.
What is your number? Hold the line.

Say ah eh-keyvoc-addoh day noomairroh. **Wrong number.**

¿Pwedoh ab-lar con el sen-yorr Perreth, pour favorr?
Please may I speak to Mr Perez?

Esta commooneecando.
The number is engaged.

No esta a-key en estay mo-mentoh.
He is not here at the moment.

Key-en ab-la?
Who is speaking?

Pour favorr, podreea deth-ear lay kay la sen-yorra Brown ya-mo pour tel-efonow ee pedearrlay kay ya-may ah estay noomairroh.
Could you tell him that Mrs Brown telephoned, and ask him to ring me at this number.

Feeling Ill

The *farmacia* will be able to give you advice and medicines for most minor ailments. If you see a doctor you will have to pay him on the spot. There is no free medical treatment in Spain. In case of an emergency, ask for a *médico de urgencia*.

Tengo dolor de cabeza.
Tengo dolorr day cab-etha.
I have a headache.

Tengo dolor de estómago.
Tengo dolorr day es-toma-go.
I have a stomach pain.

Tengo un resfriado.
Tengo oon resfree-addoh.
I have a cold.

Toso mucho.
Tossoh moochoh.
I am coughing a lot.

Tengo fiebre.
Tengo fee-ebbray.
I have a temperature.

Tengo ganas de vomitar.
Tengo ganass day vomee-tarr.
I feel sick.

Me he cortado.
May ay corr-tah-doh.
I have cut myself.

Me he quemado.
May ay kay-mah-doh.
I have burnt myself.

Tengo una insolación.
Tengo oona insoh-lah-theeon.
I am suffering from sunstroke.

Me ha picado (mordido) . . .
May ah pee-cah-doh (more-deedo) . . .
I have been stung or bitten by . . .

una medusa.
oona medoosa.
a jellyfish.

un erizo de mar
oon eh-reethoh day marr.
a sea-urchin.

una serpiente.
oona sairpee-entay.
a snake.

una avispa.
oona avees-pa.
a wasp.

Tengo algo en el ojo.
Tengo algo en el oh-hoe.
I have something in my eye.

Tengo una erupción.
Tengo oona eh-roop-theeon.
I have a rash.

Me pica.
May pee-ca.
It itches.

Tengo dolor de muelas.
Tengo dolorr day moo-elass.
I have toothache.

Me ha atacado un perro.
May ah ah-tackahdoh oon pearroh.
I have been attacked by a dog.

Me he roto la pierna.
May ay roh-toh la pee-airr-na.
I have broken my leg.

Going to the doctor

Necessito ver a un médico.

Nethesseetoh vairr ah oon mehdeecoh.
I need to see a doctor.

¿Cuándo está libre?

Cwandoe esta leebray?
When is he free?

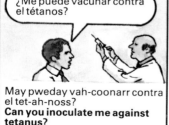
¿Me puede vacunar contra el tétanos?

May pweday vah-coonarr contra el tet-ah-noss?
Can you inoculate me against tetanus?

¿Puede recetarme algo?

Pweday rehthettarr-may algo?
Can you give me a prescription?

Parts of the Body

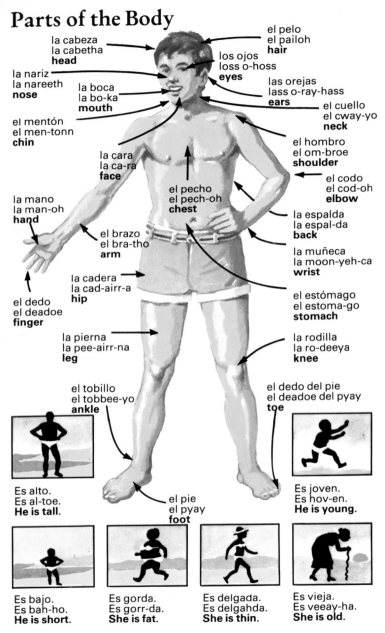

el pelo
el pailoh
hair

la cabeza
la cabetha
head

los ojos
loss o-hoss
eyes

la nariz
la nareeth
nose

la boca
la bo-ka
mouth

las orejas
lass o-ray-hass
ears

el mentón
el men-tonn
chin

el cuello
el cway-yo
neck

la cara
la ca-ra
face

el hombro
el om-broe
shoulder

el pecho
el pech-oh
chest

el codo
el cod-oh
elbow

la mano
la man-oh
hand

la espalda
la espal-da
back

el brazo
el bra-tho
arm

la muñeca
la moon-yeh-ca
wrist

el dedo
el deadoe
finger

la cadera
la cad-airr-a
hip

el estómago
el estoma-go
stomach

la pierna
la pee-airr-na
leg

la rodilla
la ro-deeya
knee

el tobillo
el tobbee-yo
ankle

el dedo del pie
el deadoe del pyay
toe

el pie
el pyay
foot

Es alto.
Es al-toe.
He is tall.

Es joven.
Es hov-en.
He is young.

Es bajo.
Es bah-ho.
He is short.

Es gorda.
Es gorr-da.
She is fat.

Es delgada.
Es delgahda.
She is thin.

Es vieja.
Es veeay-ha.
She is old.

52

Colours
Colores (Col-orress)

negro
neg-roe
black

blanco
blang-coe
white

gris
grease
grey

color arena
collaw a-rain-a
beige

marrón
ma-rron
brown

amarillo
amma-reeyo
yellow

naranja
na-ranha
orange

rojo
roh-ho
red

rosa
ross-a
pink

violeta
veeol-etta
violet

azul
a-thool
blue

verde
vairrday
green

oro
orow
gold

plata
platta
silver

oscuro
os-cure-o
dark

claro
cla-roe
light

Months, Seasons and Days

Enero
En-airroh
January

Febrero
Febrair-roe
February

Marzo
Marr-thoe
March

Abril
Ab-reel
April

Mayo
My-yo
May

Junio
Hoon-y-oh
June

Julio
Hool-y-oh
July

Agosto
A-goss-toe
August

Septiembre
Septee-embray
September

Octubre
Octoobray
October

Noviembre
Novee-embray
November

Diciembre
Deethee-embray
December

La Semana (La Sem-ahna)

7 lunes
looness
Monday

8 martes
marrtess
Tuesday

9 miércoles
me-airr-coless
Wednesday

10 jueves
hoo-evess
Thursday

11 viernes
vee-airness
Friday

12 sábado
sa-baddoh
Saturday

13 domingo
doming-goh
Sunday

La primavera
La preemavair-ra
The spring

El verano
El vair-anno
The summer

El otoño
El o-tonn-yo
The autumn

El invierno
El invee-airrno
The winter

The Weather

El Tiempo
Ell Tea-empoh

Llueve.
You-evay.
It's raining.

Va a llover.
Va ah yov-airr.
It's going to rain.

Graniza.
Gran-eetha.
It's hailing.

Hace viento.
A-thay vee-entoh.
It's windy.

Nieva.
Knee-eva.
It's snowing.

Está nublado.
Esta noo-bladoh.
It's cloudy.

Truena.
True-ayna.
It's thundering.

Un relámpago.
Oon rel-am-pagoh.
A flash of lightning.

Hace fresco.
A-thay frescoh.
It's cool.

Hace bueno.
A-thay booenoh.
It's a nice day.

Hace calor.
A-thay calorr.
It's hot.

Hace frío.
A-thay free-oh.
It's cold.

Numbers

1	Uno Oon-oh	16	Dieciséis Dee-ethee-sayeess	40	Cuarenta Cwa-renta
2	Dos Doss	17	Diecisiete Dee-ethee-see-etay	50	Cincuenta Thing-cwenta
3	Tres Tress	18	Dieciocho Dee-ethee-och-oh	60	Sesenta Sess-enta
4	Cuatro Cwatroe	19	Diecinueve Dee-ethee-noo-evay	70	Setenta Set-enta
5	Cinco Thing-co	20	Veinte Vay-intay	80	Ochenta Och-enta
6	Seis Say-eess	21	Veintiuno Vay-intee-oonoh	90	Noventa Nov-enta
7	Siete See-etay	22	Veintidós Vay-intee-doss	100	Cien Thee-en
8	Ocho Och-oh	23	Veintitrés Vay-intee-tress	101	Ciento uno Thee-entoh oonoh
9	Nueve Noo-evay	24	Veinticuatro Vay-intee-cwatroe	200	Doscientos (as) * Doss-thee-entoss (ass)*
10	Diez Dee-eth	25	Veinticinco Vay-intee-thingco	1,000	Mil Meal
11	Once Onthay	26	Veintiséis Vay-intee-say-eess	1,001	Mil uno Meal oonoh
12	Doce Dothay	27	Veintisiete Vay-intee-see-etay	2,000	Dos mil Doss meal
13	Trece Trethay	28	Veintiocho Vay-intee-och-oh	1,000,000	Un millón Oon meal-yon
14	Catorce Catorrthay	29	Veintinueve Vay-intee-noo-evay	1st	Primero (a)* Premairroh (a) *
15	Quince Kinthay	30	Treinta Tray-inta	2nd	Segundo (a)* Segoondo (a) *

*This shows the ending to use with a feminine word.

57

The Time

In Spain the 24 hour clock is used, so times after midday are written as 1300, 1400 and so on. Another point to remember is that the Spanish say, for example, "it is nine minus ten", instead of "ten minutes to nine", as we do.

¿Qué hora es, por favor?

Kay orra ess, pour favorr?
What time is it please?

Son las ocho.
Sonn lass och-oh.
It is eight o'clock.

Son las ocho y cuarto.
Sonn lass och-oh ee cwarto.
It is quarter past eight.

Son las nueve menos cuarto.
Sonn lass noo-evay menoss cwarto.
It is quarter to nine.

Es el mediodía.
Ess el meddy-oh-deea.
It is midday.

Son las cinco menos cinco.
Sonn lass thing-co menoss thing-co.
It is five to five.

Son las siete y diez.
Sonn lass see-etay ee dee-eth.
It is ten past seven.

Son las diez y media.
Sonn lass dee-eth ee meddy-a.
It is half past ten.

Es la medianoche.
Ess la meddy-a-nochay.
It is midnight.

la mañana
la man-yan-a
the morning

la tarde
la tarrday
**the afternoon and
the evening**

la noche
la nochay
the night

Time phrases

ayer ah-yair **yesterday**	este año es-tay an-yo **this year**	temprano temprahnoe **early**	dentro de cinco minutos dentro day thing-co minootoss **in five minutes**
hoy oi **today**	el mes pasado el mess pas- addoh **last month**	más temprano mass temprahnoe **earlier**	
mañana man-yan-a **tomorrow**	la semana que viene la sem-ahna kay vee-enay **next week**	pronto pronto **soon**	dentro de un cuarto de hora dentro day oon cwarto day orra **in a quarter of an hour**
anteayer antay-ah-yair **the day before yesterday**		más tarde mass tarrday **later**	
pasado mañana pas-addo man-yan-a **the day after tomorrow**	ahora a-orra **now**	nunca noonka **never**	dentro de media hora dentro day meddy-a orra **in half an hour**
			dentro de una hora dentro day oona orra **in an hour**

Basic Grammar

Nouns

All Spanish nouns are either masculine or feminine. When you learn a noun, you must learn this as well. Many nouns end with an "o", and these are nearly always masculine. Nouns ending with an "a" are usually feminine. The word for "the" is *el* before masculine (m) nouns and *la* before feminine (f) nouns.

e.g. *el libro* (the book)
la casa (the house)

If the noun is plural (p), the word for "the" is *los* before masculine nouns and *las* before feminine nouns.

e.g. *los libros* (the books)
las casas (the houses)

Spanish nouns ending with a vowel have an "s" in the plural. Nouns ending with a consonant have "es".
e.g. *la flor* (the flower)
las flores (the flowers)
la casa (the house)
las casas (the houses)

The Spanish for "a" or "an" is *un* before a masculine noun and *una* before a feminine noun.

e.g. *un libro* (a book)
una casa (a house)

Pronouns

The Spanish word for "it" or "they" depends on whether the noun it replaces is masculine or feminine.

e.g. *el gato come* (the cat eats)
él come (it eats)

In Spanish the verb can be used on its own, without the subject pronouns. Subject pronouns are used to create emphasis.

I	*yo*
you	*tú*
he, it (m)	*él*
she, if (f)	*ella*
you (polite form)	*usted*
we	*nosotros*
you (p)	*vosotros*
they (m)	*ellos*
they (f)	*ellas*
you (p) (polite form)	*ustedes*

Possessive adjectives

The word you use for "my", "you.", "his" etc. depends on whether the word that follows it is masculine, feminine or plural.

e.g. *nuestro libro* (m) (our book)
nuestra casa (f) (our house)
nuestros libros (m) (pl) (our books)

	Singular		Plural	
	(m)	**(f)**	**(m)**	**(f)**
my	mi	mi	mis	mis
your	tu	tu	tus	tus
his, her, its	su	su	sus	sus
your (polite form)				
our	nuestro	nuestra	nuestros	nuestras
your (p)	vuestro	vuestra	vuestros	vuestras
their,	su	su	sus	sus
your (p) (polite form)				

Useful verbs

There are two verbs meaning "to be" in Spanish: *ser* and *estar*. *Ser* is used to describe people and things and for telling the time. *Estar* is used to describe the position of things, such as "He is in America." and temporary conditions, such as, "It is raining."

ser	to be
yo soy	I am
tú eres	you are
él es	he is
ella es	she is
usted es	you are (polite form)
nosotros somos	we are
vosotros sois	you are (p)
ellos son	they are (m)
ellas son	they are (f)
ustedes son	you are (p) (polite form)

estar	to be
yo estoy	I am
tú estás	you are
él está	he is
ella está	she is
usted está	you are (polite form)
nosotros estamos	we are
vosotros estáis	you are (p)
ellos están	they are (m)
ellas están	they are (f)
ustedes están	you are (pl) (polite form)

tener	to have
tengo	I have
tienes	you have
tiene	he, she, it has / you have (polite form)
tenemos	we have
tenéis	you have (p)
tienen	they have / you have (p) (polite form)

hablar	to speak
hablo	I speak
hablas	you speak
habla	he, she, it speaks / you speak (polite form)
hablamos	we speak
habláis	you speak (p)
hablan	they speak / you speak (p) (polite form)

ir	to go
voy	I go
vas	you go
va	he, she, it goes / you go (polite form)
vamos	we go
vais	you go (p)
van	they go / you go (p) (polite form)

vivir	to live
vivo	I live
vives	you live
vive	he, she, it lives / you live (polite form)
vivimos	we live
vivís	you live (p)
viven	they live / you live (p) (polite form)

Negatives

To make a verb negative, add *no* before the verb.

e.g. *Hablo español*
 I speak Spanish
 No hablo español
 I do not speak Spanish

Questions . . .

There are two ways you can ask a question in Spanish. You can use your voice to make a statement sound like a question, or you can use the pronoun and put it after the verb.

e.g. *Quieres* You want
 ¿Quieres? Do you want?
 ¿Quieres tú? Do you want?

Index

This index lists some words individually and some under group names, such as food. Where you will find the Spanish for the indexed word, the page number is printed in italics, like this: *6*

Index of Spanish words

This index list some of the Spanish words you might see on signs and notices. Look up the page references to find out what they mean.